ADVANCED SET #1

RUDIMENTS EXAM SERIES

By Glory St. Germain ARCT RMT MYCC UMTC &
Shelagh McKibbon-U'Ren RMT UMTC

ULTIMATE
MUSIC THEORY

GSG MUSIC
Enriching Lives Through Music Education

ISBN: 978-1-927641-06-4

The Ultimate Music Theory™ Program

Enriching Lives Through Music Education

The Ultimate Music Theory™ Workbooks & Answer Books Program includes:

UMT Rudiments Workbooks for Prep 1, Prep 2, Basic, Intermediate, Advanced & Complete
UMT Exam Series (Set #1 & Set #2) for Preparatory, Basic, Intermediate & Advanced

Supplemental Workbooks for PREP LEVEL, LEVELS 1 - 8 & COMPLETE LEVEL
UMT Supplemental Exam Series for LEVEL 5, LEVEL 6, LEVEL 7 & LEVEL 8

The Ultimate Music Theory Program is the *Way to Score Success* as UMT helps students prepare for nationally recognized theory examinations including the Royal Conservatory of Music.

 Library and Archives Canada Cataloguing in Publication. UMT Workbooks & Exam Series /Glory St. Germain & Shelagh McKibbon-U'Ren. Respect Copyright. All rights reserved. GlorylandPublishing.com

Ultimate Music Theory Rudiments Exam Series

GP - EPS1	ISBN: 978-1-927641-00-2	Preparatory Rudiments Exams Set #1
GP - EPS1A	ISBN: 978-1-927641-08-8	Preparatory Exams Answers Set #1
GP - EPS2	ISBN: 978-1-927641-01-9	Preparatory Rudiments Exams Set #2
GP - EPS2A	ISBN: 978-1-927641-09-5	Preparatory Exams Answers Set #2
GP - EBS1	ISBN: 978-1-927641-02-6	Basic Rudiments Exams Set #1
GP - EBS1A	ISBN: 978-1-927641-10-1	Basic Exams Answers Set #1
GP - EBS2	ISBN: 978-1-927641-03-3	Basic Rudiments Exams Set #2
GP - EBS2A	ISBN: 978-1-927641-11-8	Basic Exams Answers Set #2
GP - EIS1	ISBN: 978-1-927641-04-0	Intermediate Rudiments Exams Set #1
GP - EIS1A	ISBN: 978-1-927641-12-5	Intermediate Exams Answers Set #1
GP - EIS2	ISBN: 978-1-927641-05-7	Intermediate Rudiments Exams Set #2
GP - EIS2A	ISBN: 978-1-927641-13-2	Intermediate Exams Answers Set #2
GP - EAS1	ISBN: 978-1-927641-06-4	Advanced Rudiments Exams Set #1
GP - EAS1A	ISBN: 978-1-927641-14-9	Advanced Exams Answers Set #1
GP - EAS2	ISBN: 978-1-927641-07-1	Advanced Rudiments Exams Set #2
GP - EAS2A	ISBN: 978-1-927641-15-6	Advanced Exams Answers Set #2

Ultimate Music Theory Supplemental Exam Series

GP-L5E	ISBN: 978-1-990358-11-1	LEVEL 5 Exams
GP-L5EA	ISBN: 978-1-990358-12-8	LEVEL 5 Exams Answers
GP-L6E	ISBN: 978-1-990358-13-5	LEVEL 6 Exams
GP-L6EA	ISBN: 978-1-990358-14-2	LEVEL 6 Exams Answers
GP-L7E	ISBN: 978-1-990358-15-9	LEVEL 7 Exams
GP-L7EA	ISBN: 978-1-990358-16-6	LEVEL 7 Exams Answers
GP-L8E	ISBN: 978-1-990358-17-3	LEVEL 8 Exams
GP-L8EA	ISBN: 978-1-990358-18-0	LEVEL 8 Exams Answers

Go to UltimateMusicTheory.com **and check out the FREE Resources**

Ultimate Music Theory FREE RESOURCES created just for you!

The **Ultimate Music Theory Exams** reinforce the **UMT Advanced Rudiments Workbook**.

Advanced Rudiments Theory Examination requirements include Intermediate Rudiments requirements plus the following:

Clefs
- Alto Clef and Tenor Clef (C Clefs)

Rhythm - Simple, Compound and Hybrid
- Time Signatures for hybrid meters (Example: $\frac{5}{4}$, $\frac{7}{8}$ and $\frac{10}{16}$)

Scales in Major and minor keys up to and including seven sharps and seven flats
- Write or identify: Major and minor (natural, harmonic and melodic) scales, ascending and descending, beginning on any scale degree
- Write or identify: Modes (Dorian, Phrygian, Lydian, Mixolydian and Aeolian), beginning on any note

Chords
- Write or identify: all triads (Major, minor, Augmented and diminished) in root position and inversions (close position or open position)
- Write or identify: Dominant 7th chords in Major and minor keys in root position and inversions (close position or open position)
- Write or identify: diminished 7th chords of harmonic minor scales, root position only
- Identify: the scale (Major, natural minor or harmonic minor) in which a group of triads or chords may be found

Intervals - Perfect, Major and minor
- Write or identify: above or below a given note, all intervals and their inversions, melodic or harmonic form (with or without a Key Signature), including simple intervals, compound intervals and enharmonic equivalents

Transposition (Major and minor keys up to and including seven sharps and seven flats)
- Transpose a melody up or down any interval within the octave
- Rewrite a melody at the same pitch in an alternate clef (including C Clefs)
- Transpose to concert pitch a single line of music for the following orchestral instruments: Clarinet in B flat, Trumpet in B flat, French Horn in F or English Horn in F

Cadences in all Major and harmonic minor keys
- Identify the following cadences:
    Perfect (Authentic): V - I or V^7 - I (Major) and V - i or V^7 - i (minor); Plagal: IV - I (Major) and iv - i (minor); Imperfect (Half Cadence): I - V or IV - V (Major) and i - V or iv - V (minor)
- Write the following cadences in keyboard style at the end of a melodic fragment:
    Perfect (Authentic): V - I (Major) and V - i (minor); Plagal: IV - I (Major) and iv - i (minor); Imperfect (Half Cadence): I - V or IV - V (Major) and i - V or iv - V (minor)

Scores
- Rewrite a given passage into modern vocal score, string quartet score or short score (on 2 staves)

Musical Terms and Signs
- Recognize, define or supply the musical terms or signs as listed in the Advanced Rudiments Workbook

Analysis
- Analyze a short musical composition, identifying any of the above theory requirements

Score:
60 - 69 Pass; **70 - 79** Honors; **80 - 89** First Class Honors; **90 - 100** First Class Honors with Distinction

Ultimate Music Theory: *The Way to Score Success!*

UltimateMusicTheory.com © Copyright 2013 Gloryland Publishing. All Rights Reserved.

ULTIMATE MUSIC THEORY
ADVANCED EXAM SET #1 - EXAM #1

Total Score: ____ / 100

> ♪ **UMT Tip:** Before beginning your exam, write out the Circle of Fifths. Write the order of flats and sharps. Write the Major keys on the outside of the circle and the relative minor keys on the inside of the circle.

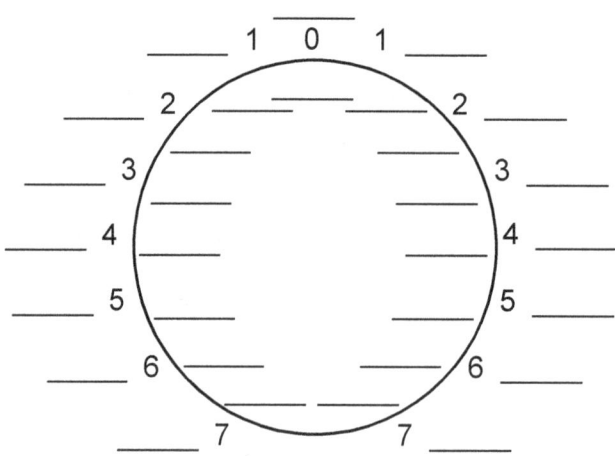

> ♪ **UMT Tip:** A Compound Interval (an interval larger than a Perfect 8) is inverted by either moving the bottom note up two octaves, moving the top note down two octaves or moving the bottom note up one octave AND moving the top note down one octave.

1. a) Write the following harmonic intervals below each of the given notes. Use whole notes.

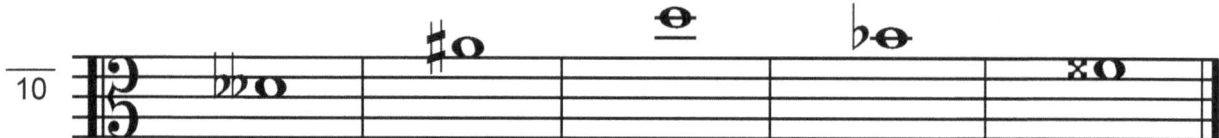

    diminished 5   Augmented 9   Major 14   minor 7   Perfect 15

   b) Invert the above harmonic intervals in the same clef. Use whole notes. Name the inversions.

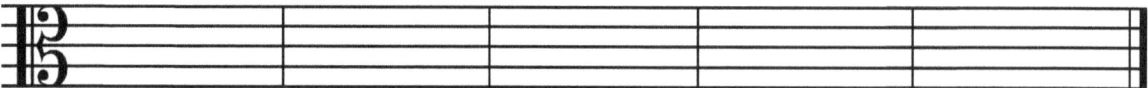

UltimateMusicTheory.com © Copyright 2013 Gloryland Publishing. All Rights Reserved.

ULTIMATE MUSIC THEORY
ADVANCED EXAM SET #1 - EXAM #1

> ♪ **UMT Tip:** The Dominant seventh chord of a minor key contains the raised 7th (raised Leading Note) of the harmonic minor scale.

2. a) Write the following solid chords in close position in the Treble Clef. Use the correct Key Signature and any necessary accidentals. Use whole notes.

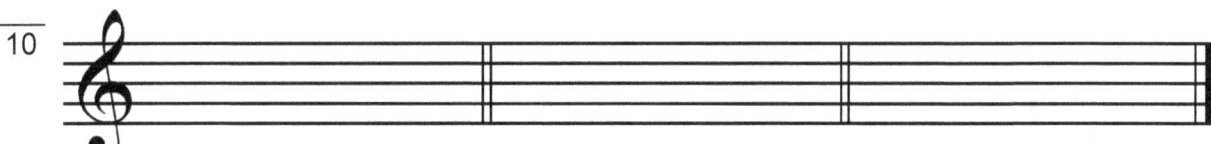

      Dominant seventh   diminished seventh   Dominant seventh
      of G Major   of b flat minor harmonic   of E flat Major
      in second inversion   in root position   in third inversion

b) Write the following solid chords in close position in the Bass Clef. Use accidentals. Use whole notes.

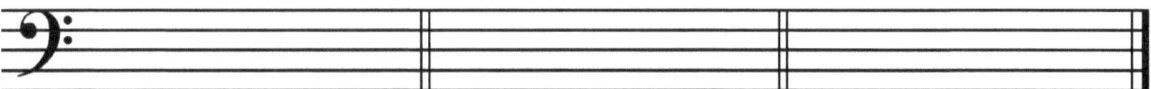

      diminished seventh   Dominant seventh   Dominant seventh
      of b minor harmonic   of c minor harmonic   of E Major
      in root position   in second inversion   in first inversion

> ♪ **UMT Tip:** The root of the diminished seventh chord of a minor key is the raised 7th (raised Leading Note) of the harmonic minor scale.

c) For each of the following seventh chords, name the type (Dominant seventh or diminished seventh) and the key to which it belongs.

Type: _____ _____ _____ _____

Key: _____ _____ _____ _____

ULTIMATE MUSIC THEORY
ADVANCED EXAM SET #1 - EXAM #1

> ♪ **UMT Tip:** A Major key will transpose to a Major key; a minor key will transpose to a minor key.

3. a) Name the key of the following melody.
   b) Transpose the melody UP an Augmented fourth, using the correct Key Signature. Name the new key.

___
10

Key: _____

Key: _____

> ♪ **UMT Tip:** The words Trumpet and Clarinet both end with the 2 letters **et**.
> "Hint": the instruments with **et** on the end go **DOWN** a Major 2.

The following melody is written for Clarinet in B flat.
c) Name the key in which it is written.
d) Transpose it to concert pitch, using the correct Key Signature. Name the new key.

Key: _____

Key: _____

UltimateMusicTheory.com © Copyright 2013 Gloryland Publishing. All Rights Reserved.

ULTIMATE MUSIC THEORY
ADVANCED EXAM SET #1 - EXAM #1

> ♪ **UMT Tip:** Scales may be written with or without a center bar line after the highest note. Either way is correct.

4. Write the following scales, ascending and descending, using the correct Key Signature and any necessary accidentals for each. Use whole notes.

$\overline{10}$ a) f sharp minor natural scale in the Treble Clef, from Supertonic to Supertonic.

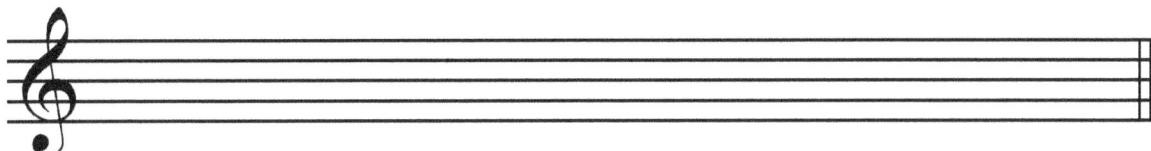

b) C sharp Major scale in the Tenor Clef, from Mediant to Mediant.

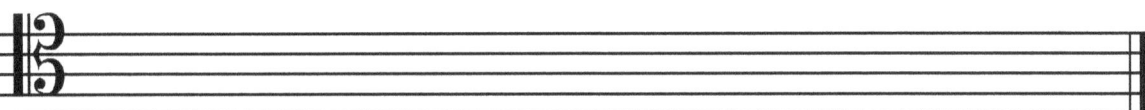

c) g minor melodic scale, in the Bass Clef, from Submediant to Submediant.

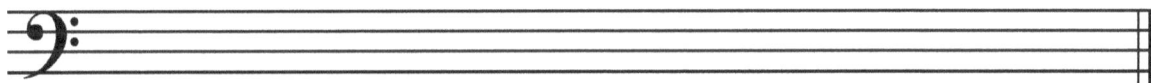

d) Dorian mode starting on D, in the Treble Clef. Use any standard notation.

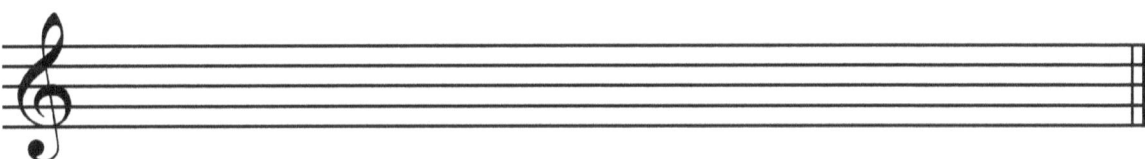

e) Whole tone scale starting on B flat, in the Bass Clef. Use any standard notation.

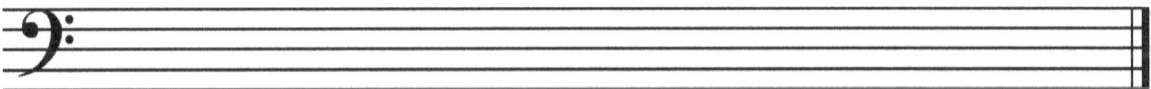

UltimateMusicTheory.com © Copyright 2013 Gloryland Publishing. All Rights Reserved.

ULTIMATE MUSIC THEORY
ADVANCED EXAM SET #1 - EXAM #1

> ♪ **UMT Tip:** Always write the cadence under the given notes. Use the same note values as the given notes. For dotted notes, a dot must be written beside each note in the cadence. The dot is always written to the right of the notehead - in the space above the line for a line note and in the space beside the notehead for a space note.

5. For each of the following melodic fragments:
   a) Name the key.
   b) Write a cadence in keyboard style below the notes underneath the brackets.
   c) Name the type of cadence (Perfect, Imperfect or Plagal).

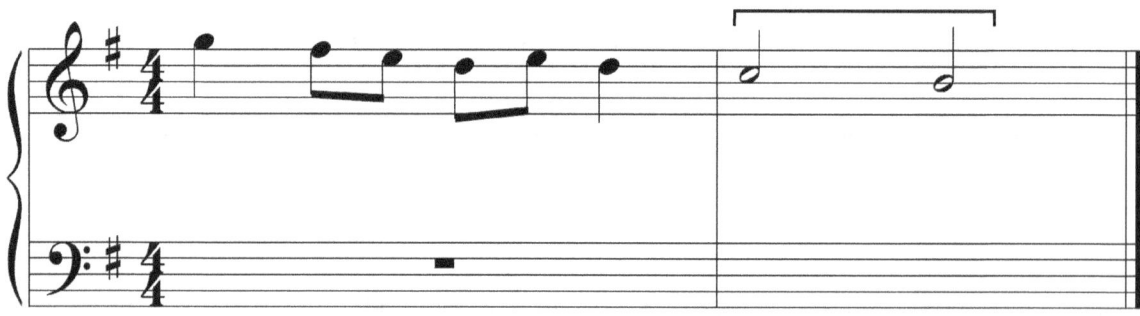

Key: _____   _____

Key: _____   _____

ULTIMATE MUSIC THEORY
ADVANCED EXAM SET #1 - EXAM #1

♪ **UMT Tip:** Use the proper clefs for each open score.

6. For each of the following chords:
   a) Name the chord type as: triad, Dominant seventh chord, diminished seventh chord, cluster or quartal chord.
   b) Rewrite the chord in the specified type of open score.
   c) Name each voice/instrument in the open score. Do not use abbreviations.

/10

Modern Vocal Score

Chord Type: _____

Open Score for String Quartet

Chord Type: _____

ULTIMATE MUSIC THEORY
ADVANCED EXAM SET #1 - EXAM #1

> ♪ **UMT Tip:** Write the Basic Beat and Pulse below each measure for simple, compound or hybrid time. Cross off the Basic Beat as each beat is completed.

7. Add rests below each bracket to complete each measure.

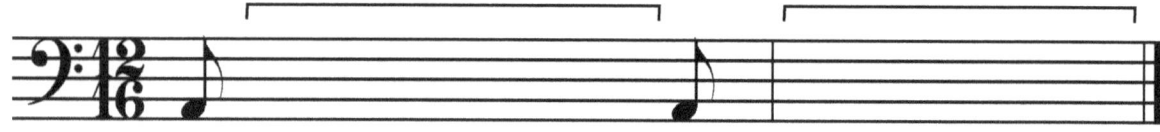

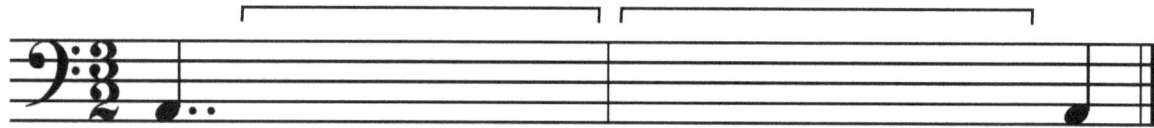

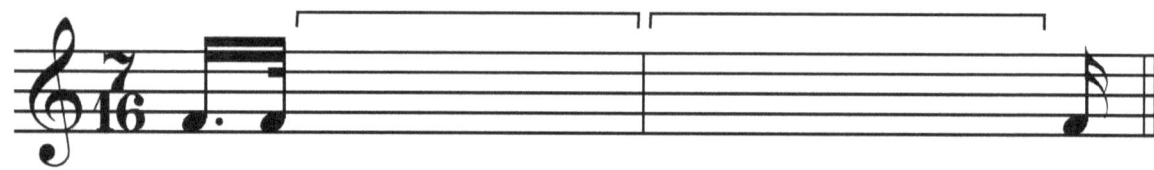

ULTIMATE MUSIC THEORY
ADVANCED EXAM SET #1 - EXAM #1

♪ **UMT Tip:** The quality/type of a triad is Major, minor, Augmented or diminished.

8. a) For each of the following close position triads, identify the root note, the quality/type and the position.

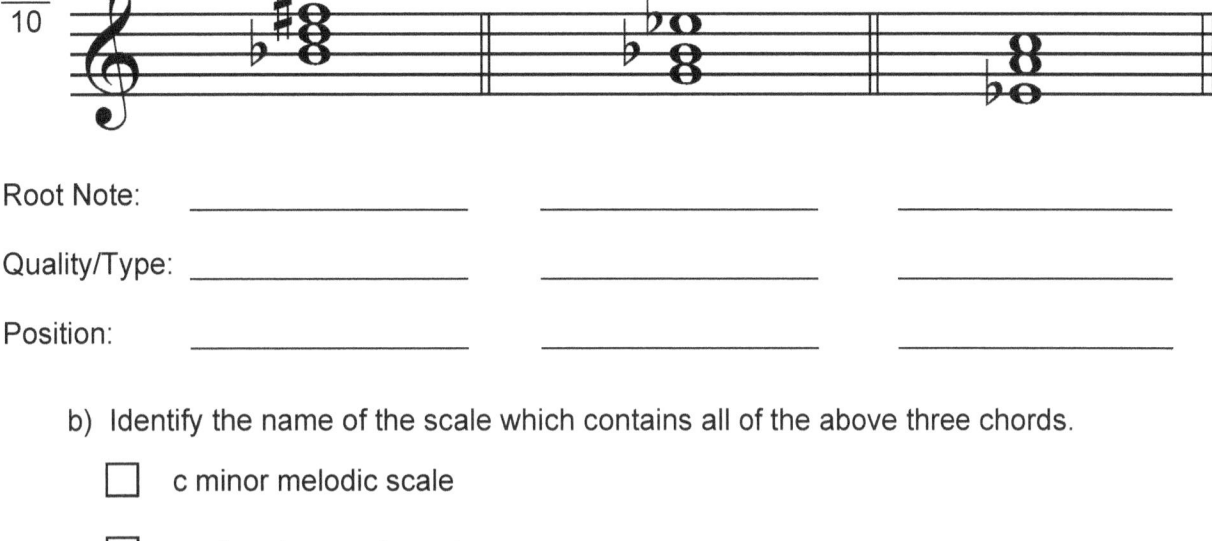

Root Note: _____   _____   _____

Quality/Type: _____   _____   _____

Position: _____   _____   _____

b) Identify the name of the scale which contains all of the above three chords.

☐ c minor melodic scale

☐ g minor harmonic scale

☐ D Major scale

c) Write each of the following open position triads in close position inside the square brackets. Use whole notes.

d) Identify the root note, the quality/type and the position.

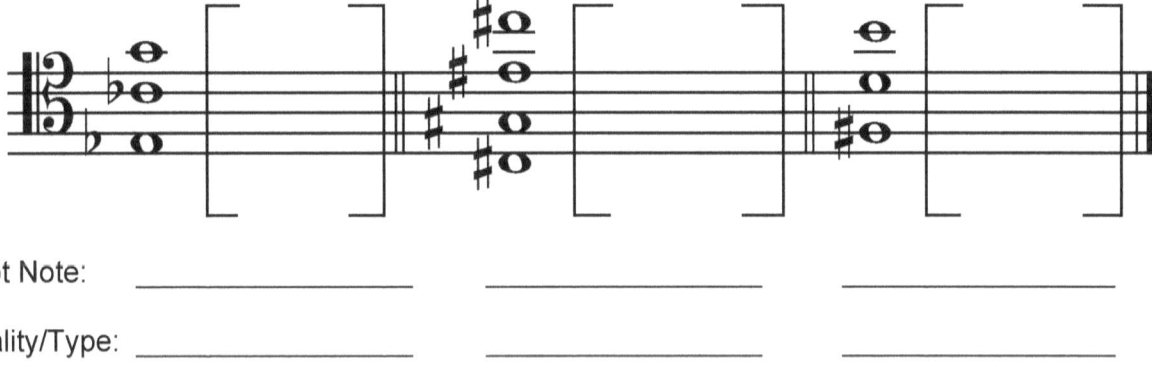

Root Note: _____   _____   _____

Quality/Type: _____   _____   _____

Position: _____   _____   _____

UltimateMusicTheory.com © Copyright 2013 Gloryland Publishing. All Rights Reserved.

ULTIMATE MUSIC THEORY
ADVANCED EXAM SET #1 - EXAM #1

♪ **UMT Tip:** Musical terms can be in French, German or Italian.

9. Give the English meaning for the following musical terms.

___
10

	Term	Definition
a)	*stringendo*	_____
b)	*schnell*	_____
c)	*vivo*	_____
d)	*risoluto*	_____
e)	*giocoso*	_____
f)	*langsam*	_____
g)	*tutti*	_____
h)	*vite*	_____
i)	*agitato*	_____
j)	*quindicesima alta*	_____

ULTIMATE MUSIC THEORY
ADVANCED EXAM SET #1 - EXAM #1

♪ **UMT Tip:** The relationship between musical passages can be imitation, inversion or sequence.

10. Analyze the following piece of music by answering the questions below.

Richard's Puppy

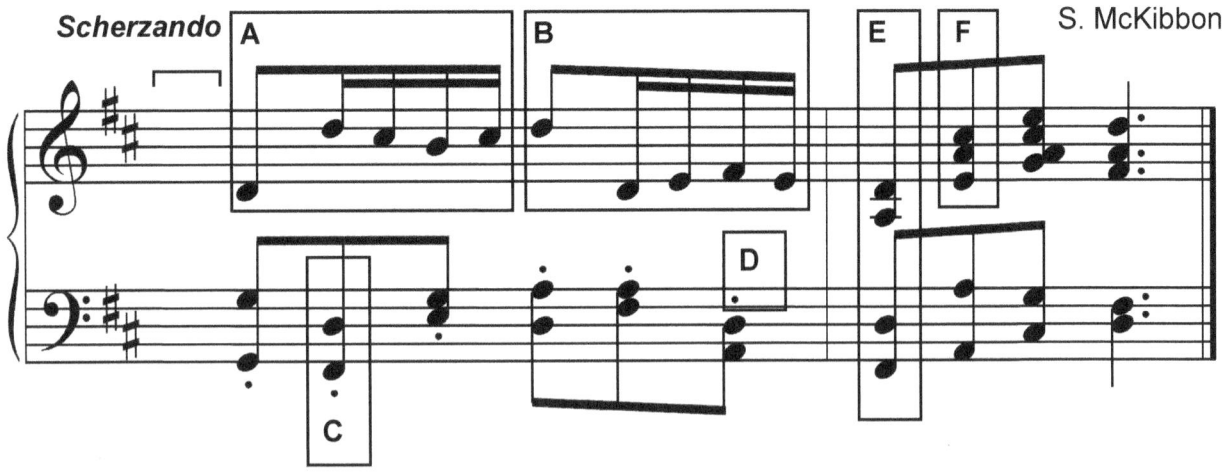

a) Name the key of this piece. _____

b) Explain the term Scherzando. _____

c) Add the Time Signature directly on the music.

d) Give the term for the relationship between the Right Hand at letters **A** and **B**. _____

e) Name the interval at the letter **C**. _____

f) Identify the sign at the letter **D**. _____

g) For the triad at **E**, name: Root: ____ Type/Quality: _____ Position: _____

h) For the triad at **F**, name: Root: ____ Type/Quality: _____ Position: _____

i) Locate and circle a Tritone. Name the interval. _____

j) Locate and circle a Dominant Seventh Chord. Label it as V^7.

ULTIMATE MUSIC THEORY
ADVANCED EXAM SET #1 - EXAM #2

Total Score: ____ / 100

♪ **UMT Tip:** Before beginning your exam, write out the Circle of Fifths. Write the order of flats and sharps. Write the Major keys on the outside of the circle and the relative minor keys on the inside of the circle.

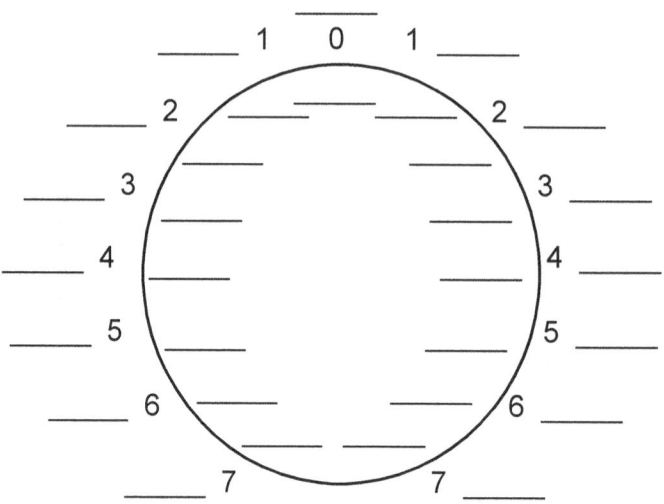

♪ **UMT Tip:** Read the instructions carefully. On the exam, the interval question may ask you to invert the intervals OR to change the upper or lower notes of each interval enharmonically. An enharmonic note (enharmonic equivalent) has the same pitch using a different letter name.

1. a) Name the following intervals.

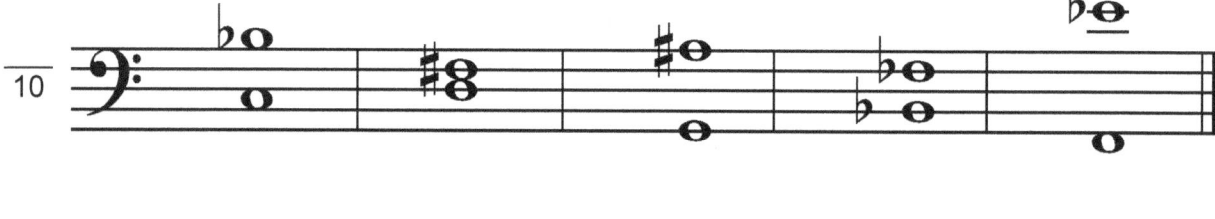

_____ _____ _____ _____ _____

b) Change the UPPER note of each interval enharmonically. Use whole notes. Rename the intervals.

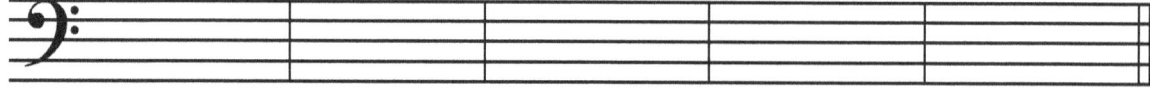

_____ _____ _____ _____ _____

UltimateMusicTheory.com © Copyright 2013 Gloryland Publishing. All Rights Reserved.

ULTIMATE MUSIC THEORY
ADVANCED EXAM SET #1 - EXAM #2

> ♪ **UMT Tip:** When writing chords using accidentals, the Dominant seventh chord of a Major key and its Tonic minor key is the same chord.

2. i) For each of the following Dominant seventh chords, name:
   a) the two keys to which it belongs.
   b) the position.

___
10

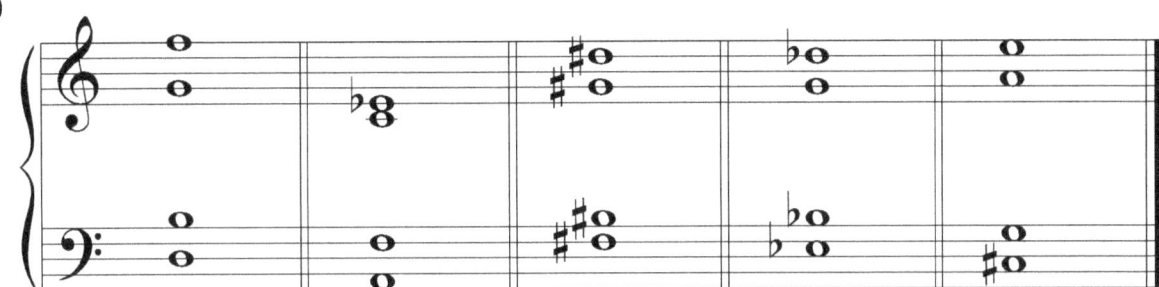

a) _____ _____ _____ _____ _____

b) _____ _____ _____ _____ _____

> ♪ **UMT Tip:** The root of the diminished seventh chord of a minor key is the raised 7th (raised Leading Note) of the harmonic minor scale.

ii) For each of the following diminished seventh chords, name:
   a) the key to which it belongs.
   b) the position.

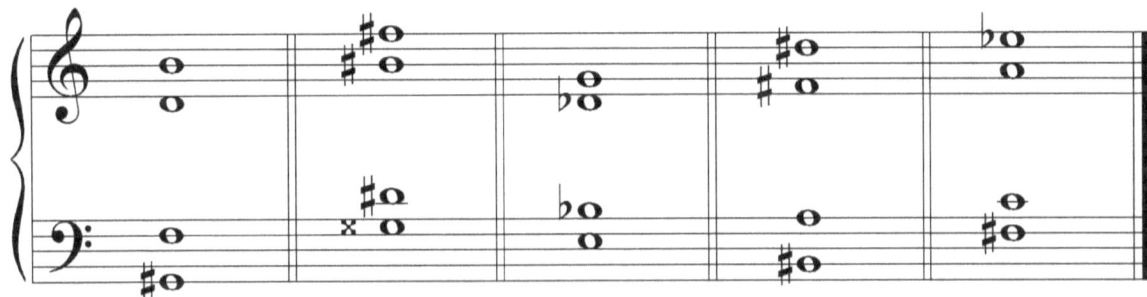

a) _____ _____ _____ _____ _____

b) _____ _____ _____ _____ _____

ULTIMATE MUSIC THEORY
ADVANCED EXAM SET #1 - EXAM #2

> ♪ **UMT Tip:** To identify the new key, draw a staff in the margin. Write the interval above or below the Tonic note of the given melody as indicated. That names the new key.

3. a) Name the key of the following melody.
   b) Transpose the melody UP a minor third, using the correct Key Signature. Name the new key.

Key: _____

Key: _____

> ♪ **UMT Tip:** The French Horn and English Horn are both Horns. "Horns" has 5 letters. "Hint": the instruments that are Horns go DOWN a Perfect 5th.

The following melody is written for French Horn in F.
c) Name the key in which it is written.
d) Transpose it to concert pitch, using the correct Key Signature. Name the new key.

Key: _____

Key: _____

ULTIMATE MUSIC THEORY
ADVANCED EXAM SET #1 - EXAM #2

> ♪ **UMT Tip:** Scales may be written with or without a center bar line. When using a center bar line, accidentals may need to be repeated in the descending scale.

4. Write the following scales, ascending and descending, using accidentals. Use whole notes.

$\overline{10}$ a) D flat Major scale in the Alto Clef, from Dominant to Dominant.

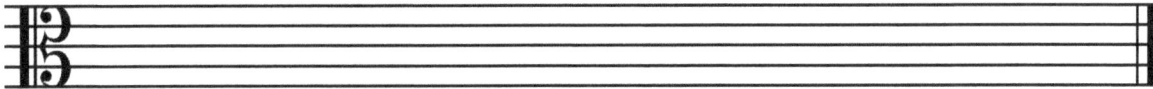

b) b minor melodic scale in the Bass Clef, from Leading note to Leading note.

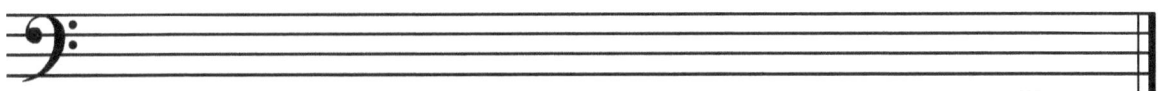

c) The enharmonic Tonic minor, natural form, of e flat minor, in the Treble Clef, from Tonic to Tonic.

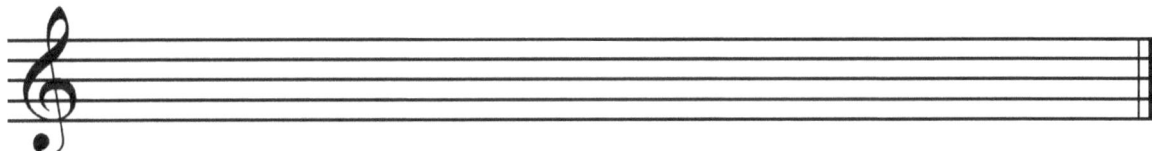

d) Lydian Mode starting on G, in the Tenor Clef. Use any standard notation.

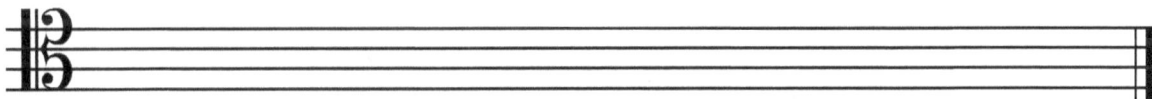

e) Whole tone scale starting on F sharp, in the Treble Clef. Use any standard notation.

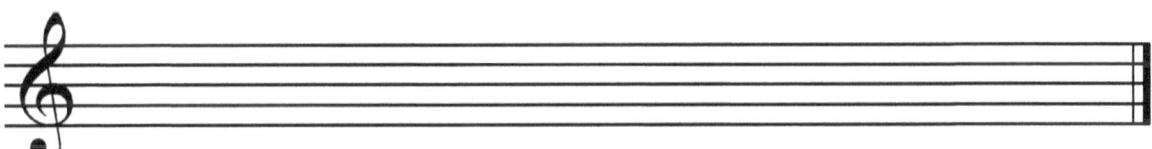

ULTIMATE MUSIC THEORY
ADVANCED EXAM SET #1 - EXAM #2

> ♪ **UMT Tip:** Functional Chord Symbols for Major keys are I, IV, V and V^7.
> Functional Chord Symbols for minor keys are i, iv, V and V^7.

5. For each of the following melodic fragments:
   a) Name the key.
   b) Use Functional Chord Symbols (Roman Numerals) to identify the Chords under the bracket.
   c) Name the type of cadence (Perfect, Imperfect or Plagal).

__10__

Key: _____   Key: _____

Chord Symbols: ____ ____   Chord Symbols: ____ ____

Cadence: _____   Cadence: _____

For the following melodic fragment:
d) Name the key.
e) Write a cadence in keyboard style below the notes underneath the bracket.
f) Name the type of cadence (Perfect, Imperfect or Plagal).

Key: _____   _____

ULTIMATE MUSIC THEORY
ADVANCED EXAM SET #1 - EXAM #2

> ♪ **UMT Tip:** Short score uses two staves (Treble and Bass).

6. The following passage is in Open Score for String Quartet.
   a) Name the instruments used (do not use abbreviations).
   b) Name the key.
   c) Rewrite the passage in Short Score.

$\overline{10}$

Key: _____

ULTIMATE MUSIC THEORY
ADVANCED EXAM SET #1 - EXAM #2

♪ **UMT Tip:** Complete the given beats first, then complete the remaining beats.

7. Add rests below each bracket to complete each measure.

___ 10

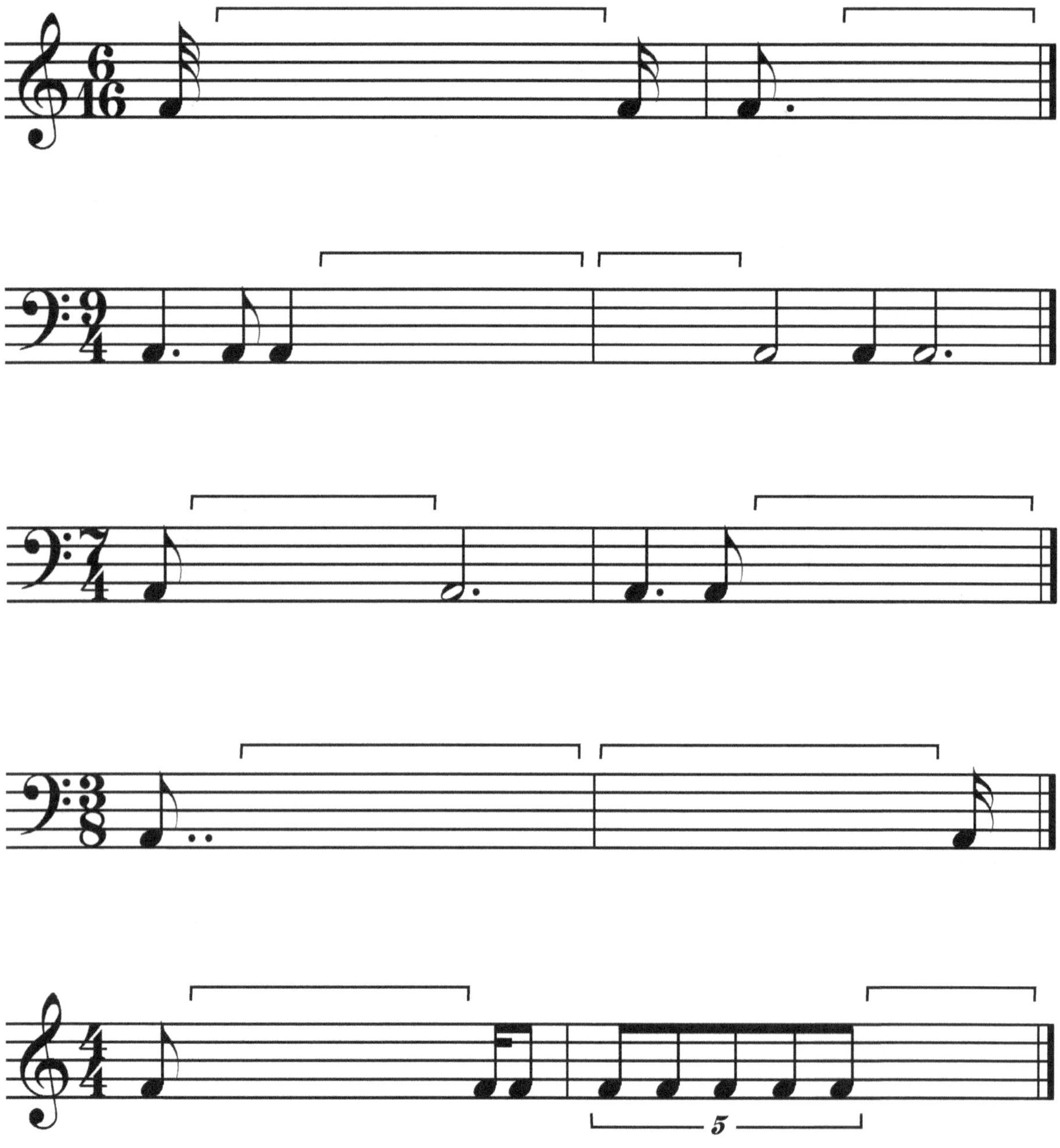

ULTIMATE MUSIC THEORY
ADVANCED EXAM SET #1 - EXAM #2

> ♪ **UMT Tip:** A quartal chord is built on intervals of fourths. A polychord is a combination of two or more different chords. A cluster chord is a chord consisting of three or more adjacent notes of a scale.

8. Name each of the following chords as a Major triad, minor triad, Augmented triad, diminished triad, Dominant seventh chord, diminished seventh chord, quartal chord, polychord or cluster chord.

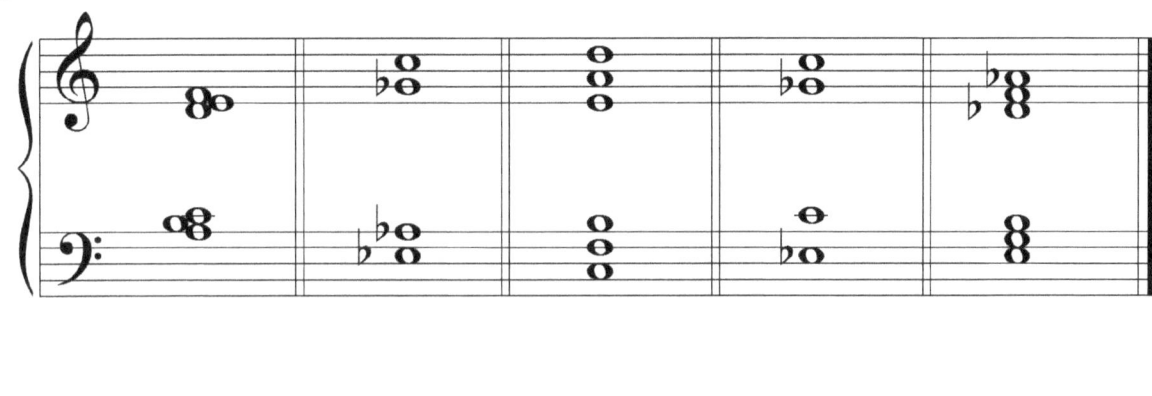

_____   _____   _____   _____   _____

_____   _____   _____   _____   _____

ULTIMATE MUSIC THEORY
ADVANCED EXAM SET #1 - EXAM #2

> ♪ **UMT Tip:** Before looking at the possible definitions, look at the Term and identify the definition. Then match the definition with one one of the given definitions.

9. Match each musical term with its English definition. (Not all definitions will be used.)

$\overline{10}$

Term		Definition
léger	_____	a) turn the page quickly
comodo	_____	b) be silent
sopra	_____	c) moderate, moderately
tacet	_____	d) at a comfortable, easy tempo
volti subito	_____	e) simple
calando	_____	f) at the liberty of the performer
semplice	_____	g) above
arco	_____	h) with fire
mässig	_____	i) light, lightly
con fuoco	_____	j) becoming slower and softer
		k) for stringed instruments: resume bowing after a pizzicato passage

UltimateMusicTheory.com © Copyright 2013 Gloryland Publishing. All Rights Reserved.

ULTIMATE MUSIC THEORY
ADVANCED EXAM SET #1 - EXAM #2

♪ **UMT Tip:** The relationship between musical passages can be imitation, inversion or sequence.

10. Analyze the following piece of music by answering the questions below.

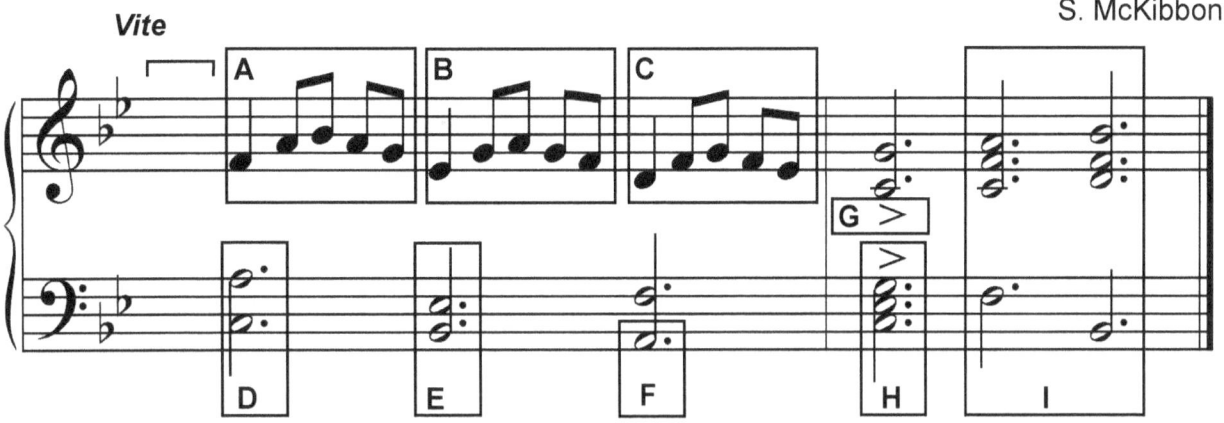

Deanna's Dance
S. McKibbon

a) Name the key of this piece. _____

b) Explain the tempo of this piece. _____

c) Add the Time Signature directly on the music.

d) Give the term for the relationship between the Right Hand at letters **A, B** and **C**. _____

e) Name the interval at the letter **D**. _____

f) Name the interval at the letter **E**. _____

g) Identify the technical degree for the note at the letter **F**. _____

h) Explain the sign at the letter **G**. _____

i) For the triad at **H**, name: Root: _____ Type/Quality: _____ Position: _____

j) Identify the cadence at the letter **I**. _____

ULTIMATE MUSIC THEORY
ADVANCED EXAM SET #1 - EXAM #3

Total Score: ____
100

1. a) Name the following intervals.

_____ _____ _____ _____ _____

b) Invert the above melodic intervals in the same clef. Name the inversions.

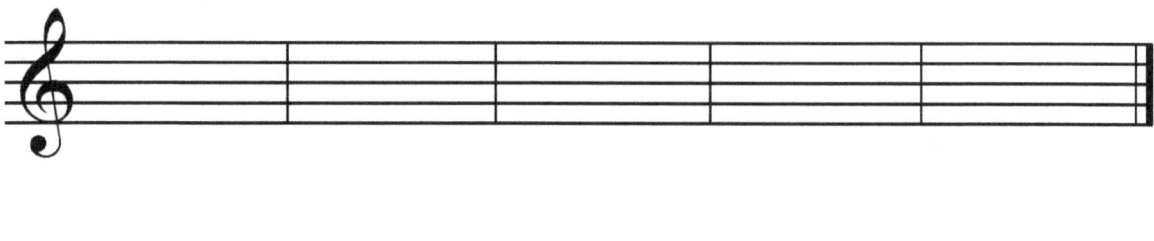

_____ _____ _____ _____ _____

c) Write the following harmonic intervals below each of the given notes. Use whole notes.

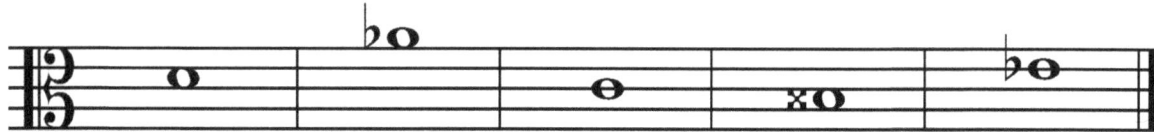

minor 3   Perfect 8   diminished 6   Augmented 2   Major 7

d) Invert the above harmonic intervals in the same clef. Name the inversions.

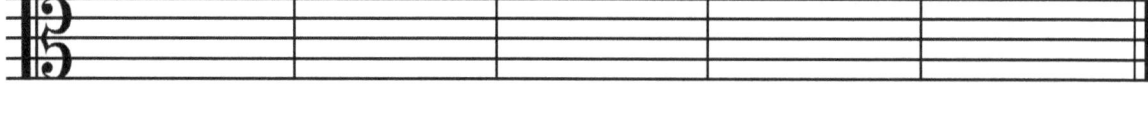

_____ _____ _____ _____ _____

UltimateMusicTheory.com © Copyright 2013 Gloryland Publishing. All Rights Reserved.

ULTIMATE MUSIC THEORY
ADVANCED EXAM SET #1 - EXAM #3

2. a) For each of the following chords, name the root, the type/quality (Major, minor, Augmented or diminished) and the position.

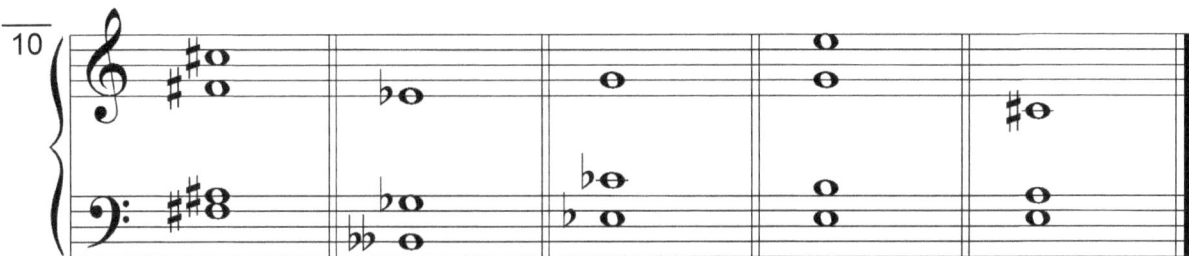

Root: _____ _____ _____ _____ _____

Type: _____ _____ _____ _____ _____

Position: _____ _____ _____ _____ _____

b) For each of the following Dominant Seventh chords, name the two keys to which it belongs and name the position.

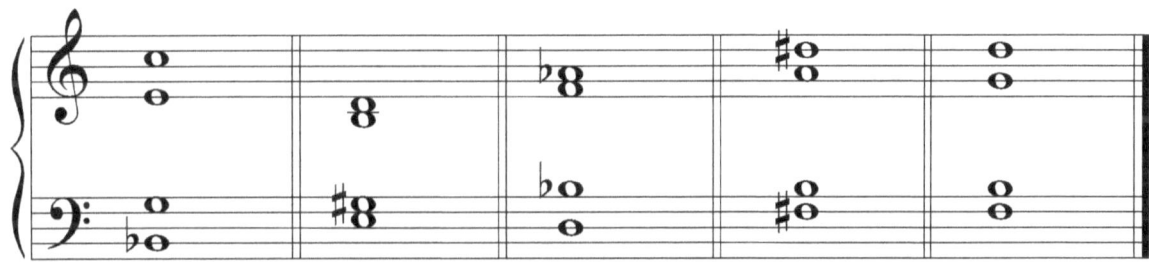

Major key: _____ _____ _____ _____ _____

Minor key: _____ _____ _____ _____ _____

Position: _____ _____ _____ _____ _____

3. a) Name the key of the following melody.
   b) Rewrite the melody at the same pitch in the Bass Clef.

Key: _____

The following melody is written for Clarinet in B flat.
c) Name the key in which it is written.
d) Transpose it to concert pitch, using the correct Key Signature. Name the new key.

Key: _____

Key: _____

ULTIMATE MUSIC THEORY
ADVANCED EXAM SET #1 - EXAM #3

4. Add the proper clef, Key Signature and any necessary accidentals, in order to form the following scales.

10 a) F sharp Major scale, from Subdominant to Subdominant.

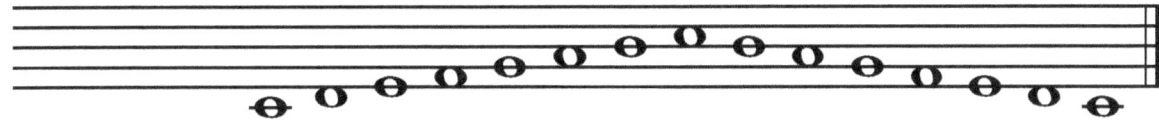

b) g sharp minor scale, melodic form, from Tonic to Tonic.

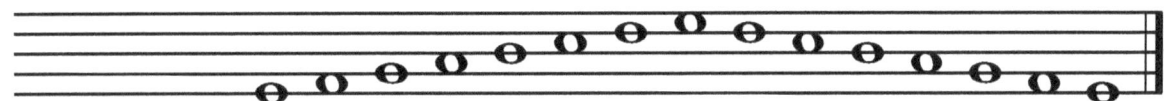

c) b flat minor scale, harmonic form, from Leading note to Leading note.

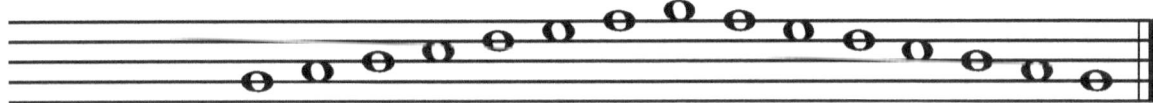

d) Phrygian mode starting on F.

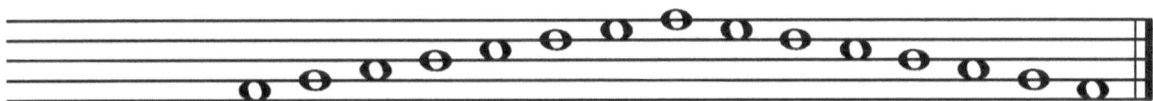

e) Aeolian mode starting on C sharp.

ULTIMATE MUSIC THEORY
ADVANCED EXAM SET #1 - EXAM #3

5. For each of the following melodic fragments:
   a) Name the key.
   b) Write the Roman Numerals below the Chords underneath the bracket.

   ___
   10 c) Name the type of cadence (Perfect, Imperfect or Plagal).

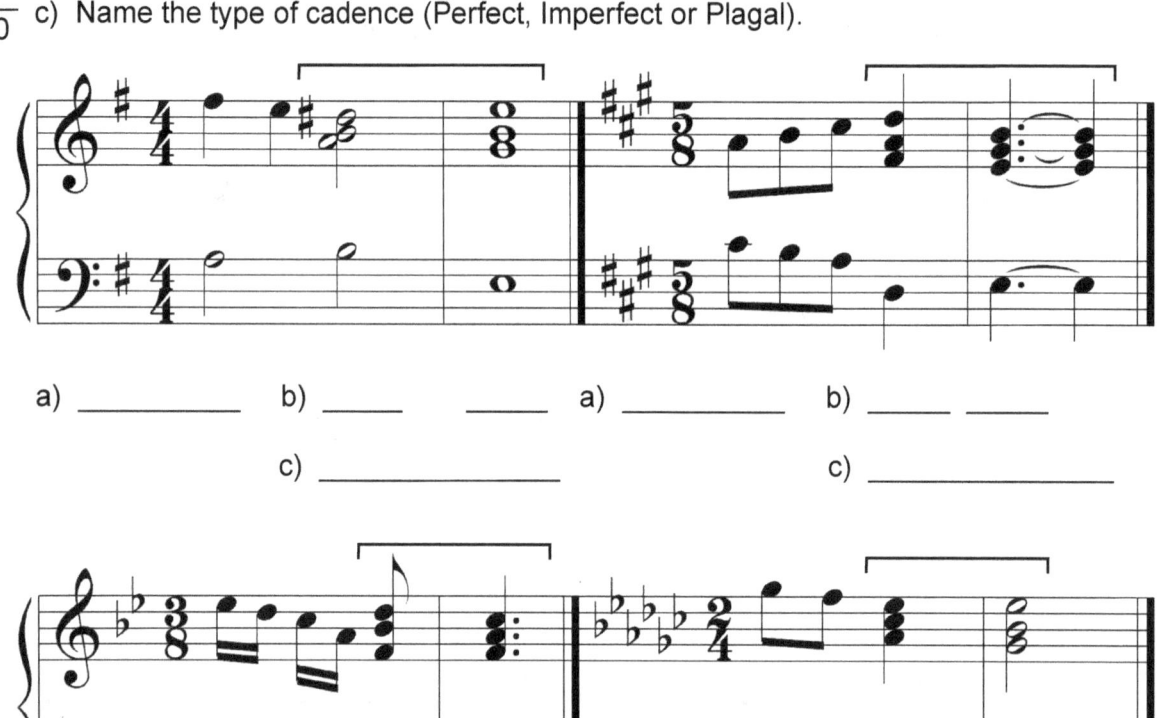

a) _____ b) ____ ____   a) _____ b) ____ ____

   c) _____   c) _____

a) _____ b) ____ ____   a) _____ b) ____ ____

   c) _____   c) _____

a) _____   b) ____ ____

                                              c) _____

ULTIMATE MUSIC THEORY
ADVANCED EXAM SET #1 - EXAM #3

6. For each of the following chords:
   a) Name the chord type as: triad, Dominant seventh chord, diminished seventh chord, cluster or quartal chord.
   b) Rewrite the chord in the specified type of open score.
   c) Name each voice/instrument in the open score. Do not use abbreviations.

$\overline{10}$

Modern Vocal Score

Chord Type:

Open Score for String Quartet

Chord Type:

ULTIMATE MUSIC THEORY
ADVANCED EXAM SET #1 - EXAM #3

7. Add rests below each bracket to complete each measure.

ULTIMATE MUSIC THEORY
ADVANCED EXAM SET #1 - EXAM #3

8. a) Name the following as blues scale, Major pentatonic scale, minor pentatonic scale, octatonic scale, whole tone (whole step) scale or chromatic scale.

b) Name each of the following chords as Dominant seventh chord, diminished seventh chord, quartal chord, polychord or cluster chord.

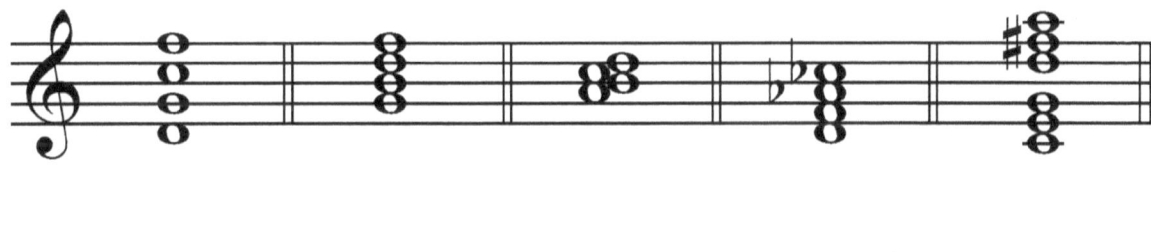

_____ _____ _____ _____ _____

ULTIMATE MUSIC THEORY
ADVANCED EXAM SET #1 - EXAM #3

9. Give the English definition for TEN of the following musical terms.

Term	Definition
sonore	_____
mouvement	_____
sehr	_____
attacca	_____
grandioso	_____
pesante	_____
subito	_____
cédez	_____
dolente	_____
morendo	_____
con sordino	_____
martellato	_____

ULTIMATE MUSIC THEORY
ADVANCED EXAM SET #1 - EXAM #3

10. Analyze the following musical excerpt by answering the questions below.

Minuet in F

W. A. Mozart

Maestoso

a) Name the key of this piece. _____

b) Explain the term Maestoso. _____

c) Add the Time Signature directly on the music.

d) Add the correct rest at the letter **A**.

e) Name the intervals at the letters: **B** _____ **C** _____

f) Identify the technical degree for the note at the letter **D**. _____

g) For the triad at **E**, name: Root: ____ Type/Quality: _____ Position: _____

h) For the triad at **F**, name: Root: ____ Type/Quality: _____ Position: _____

i) Name the notes at the letters: **G** _____ **H** _____

j) For the triad at **I**, name: Root: ____ Type/Quality: _____ Position: _____

UltimateMusicTheory.com © Copyright 2013 Gloryland Publishing. All Rights Reserved.

ULTIMATE MUSIC THEORY
ADVANCED EXAM SET #1 - EXAM #4

Total Score: ____
/100

1. a) Name the following intervals.

_____ _____ _____ _____ _____

b) Invert the above melodic intervals in the same clef. Use whole notes. Name the inversions.

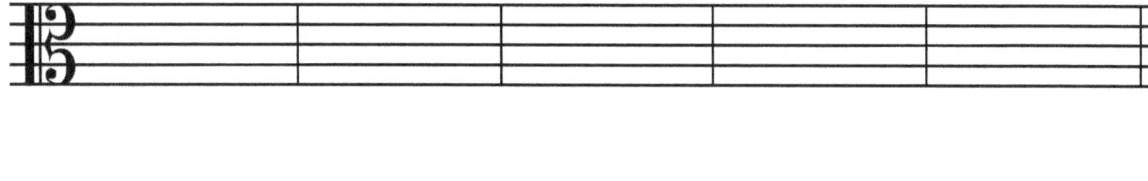

_____ _____ _____ _____ _____

c) Write the following harmonic intervals above each of the given notes. Use whole notes.

Major 10   Perfect 8   diminished 11   Augmented 4   Major 7

d) Invert the above harmonic intervals in the same clef. Use whole notes. Name the inversions.

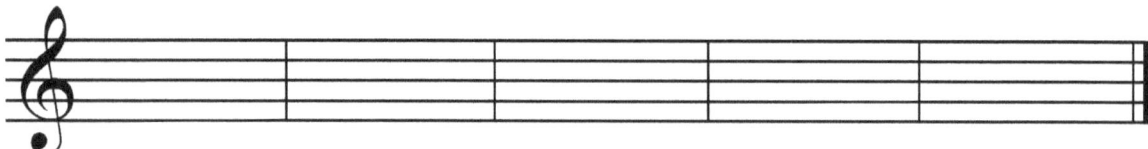

_____ _____ _____ _____ _____

UltimateMusicTheory.com © Copyright 2013 Gloryland Publishing. All Rights Reserved.

ULTIMATE MUSIC THEORY
ADVANCED EXAM SET #1 - EXAM #4

2. Write the following chords in the Treble Clef. Use accidentals. Use whole notes.

   a) The Dominant seventh chord of A flat Major in second inversion.

__10__ b) The diminished seventh chord of g sharp minor harmonic in root position.

   c) The Dominant seventh chord of b minor harmonic in first inversion.

   d) The diminished seventh chord of c minor harmonic in root position.

   e) The Dominant seventh chord of B Major in third inversion.

    a)   b)   c)   d)   e)

2. Write the following chords in the Bass Clef. Use a Key Signature. Use whole notes.

   f) The Dominant seventh chord of G Major in third inversion.

   g) The diminished seventh chord of c sharp minor harmonic in root position.

   h) The Dominant seventh chord of e minor harmonic in second inversion.

   i) The diminished seventh chord of b minor harmonic in root position.

   j) The Dominant seventh chord of F Major in first inversion.

    f)   g)   h)   i)   j)

UltimateMusicTheory.com © Copyright 2013 Gloryland Publishing. All Rights Reserved.

3. a) Name the key of the following melody.
   b) Rewrite the melody at the same pitch in the Alto C Clef.

Key: _____

The following melody is written for Clarinet in B flat.
c) Name the key in which it is written.
d) Transpose it to concert pitch, using the correct Key Signature. Name the new key.

Key: _____

Key: _____

ULTIMATE MUSIC THEORY
ADVANCED EXAM SET #1 - EXAM #4

4. Write the following scales, ascending and descending, in the given clefs. Use a Key Signature. Use whole notes.

a) g sharp minor, melodic form, from Submediant to Submediant.

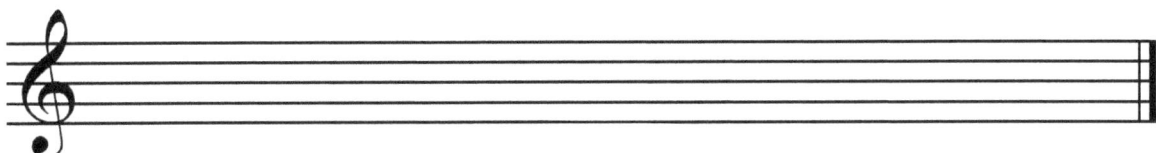

b) f minor scale, harmonic form, from Supertonic to Supertonic.

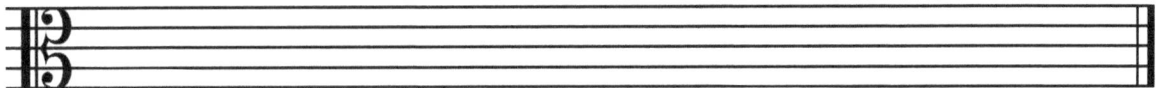

c) The relative Major of g minor, from Leading Note to Leading Note.

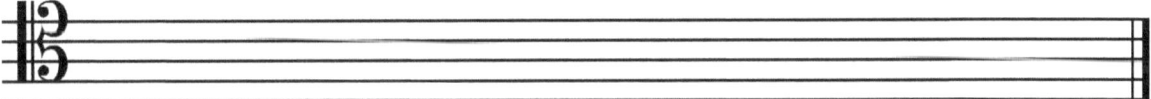

d) f sharp minor scale, natural form, from Mediant to Mediant.

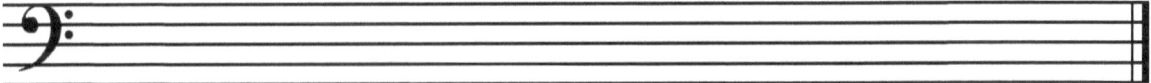

e) B Major scale, from Subdominant to Subdominant.

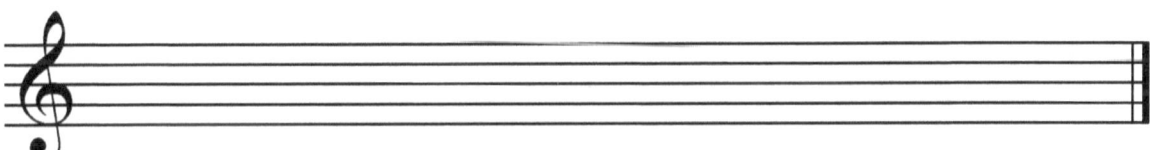

ULTIMATE MUSIC THEORY
ADVANCED EXAM SET #1 - EXAM #4

5. For each of the following melodic fragments:
   a) Name the key.
   b) Use Functional Chord Symbols (Roman Numerals) to identify the Chords under the bracket.
   c) Name the type of cadence (Perfect, Imperfect or Plagal).

___
10

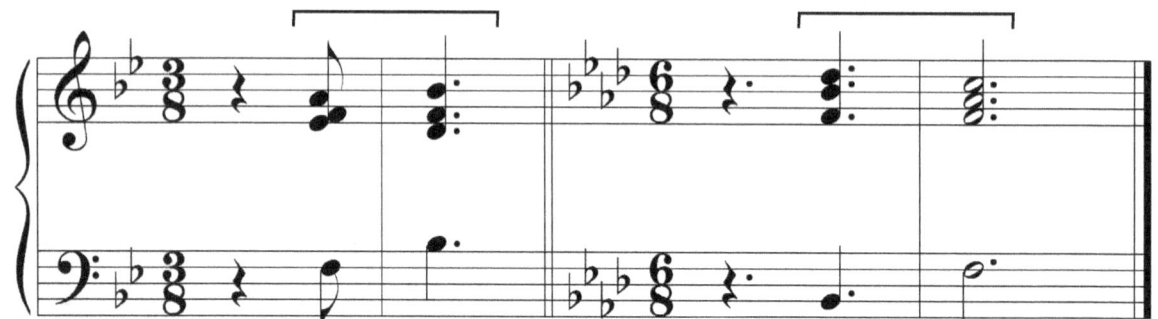

Key: _____   Key: _____

Chord Symbols: ____ ____   Chord Symbols: ____ ____

Cadence: _____   Cadence: _____

For the following melodic fragment:
d) Name the key.
e) Write a cadence in keyboard style below the notes underneath the bracket.
f) Name the type of cadence (Perfect, Imperfect or Plagal).

Key: _____   _____

ULTIMATE MUSIC THEORY
ADVANCED EXAM SET #1 - EXAM #4

6. The following melody is written in Modern Vocal Score.
   a) Name the key.
   b) Rewrite it in Short Score.

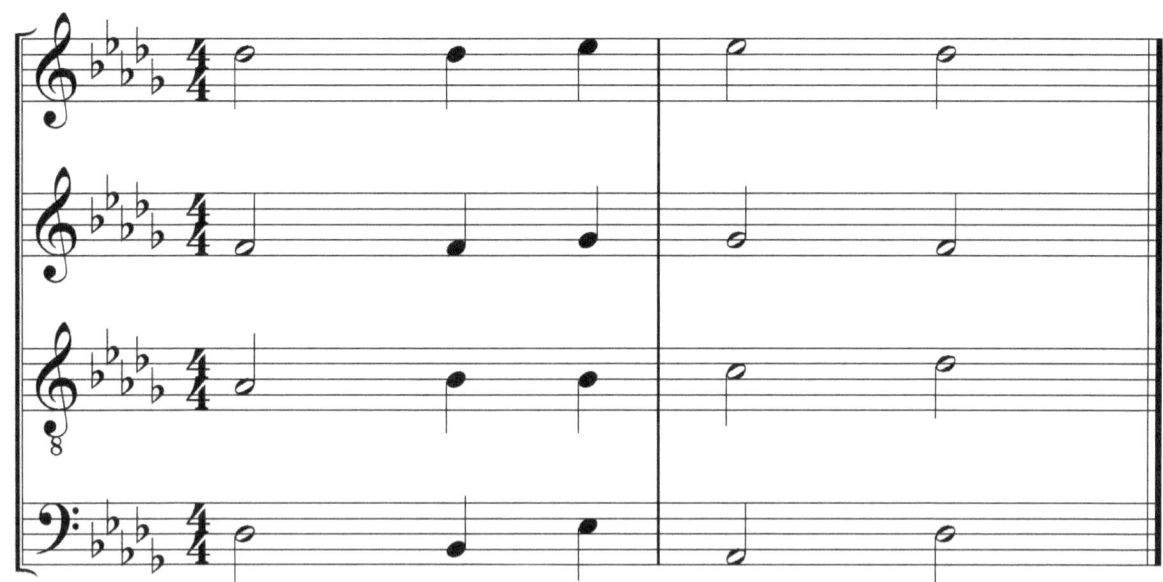

Key: _____

ULTIMATE MUSIC THEORY
ADVANCED EXAM SET #1 - EXAM #4

7. Add rests below each bracket to complete each measure.

ULTIMATE MUSIC THEORY
ADVANCED EXAM SET #1 - EXAM #4

8. a) Write the Lydian mode starting on E, ascending and descending. Use whole notes.

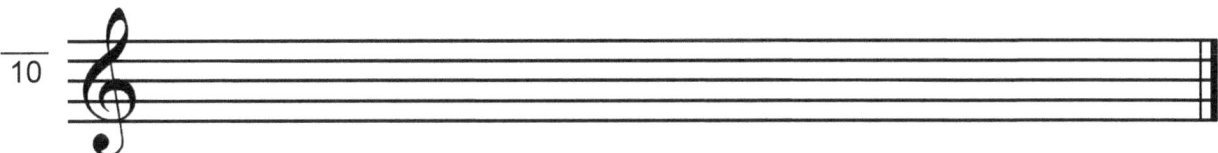

   b) Write the whole tone scale starting on E flat, ascending and descending. Use whole notes.

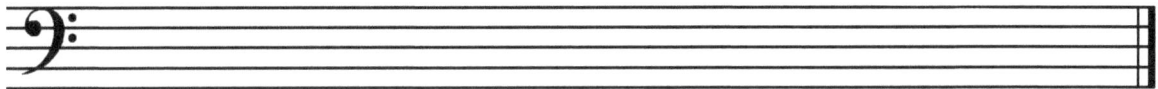

   c) Write the Phrygian mode starting on D, ascending and descending. Use whole notes.

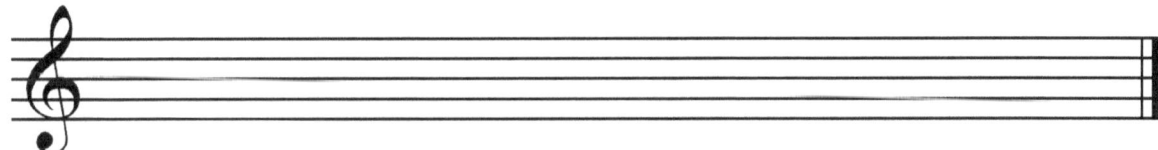

   d) Write the Mixolydian mode starting on C, ascending and descending. Use whole notes.

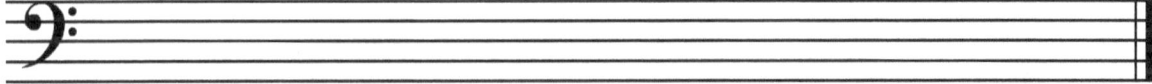

   e) Write the chromatic scale starting on G, ascending and descending. Use whole notes.

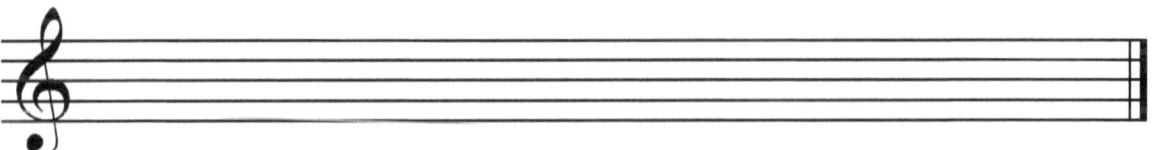

ULTIMATE MUSIC THEORY
ADVANCED EXAM SET #1 - EXAM #4

9. For each of the following triads, name:
   a) the root note.
   b) the quality (Major, minor, Augmented or diminished).

___
10

Example:

The Supertonic Triad of A flat Major	Root: B♭	Quality: minor
The Subdominant Triad of g minor harmonic	Root: _____	Quality: _____
The Submediant Triad of f sharp minor harmonic	Root: _____	Quality: _____
The Tonic Triad of B Major	Root: _____	Quality: _____
The Mediant Triad of E Major	Root: _____	Quality: _____
The Dominant Triad of a flat minor harmonic	Root: _____	Quality: _____
The Leading Note Triad of e minor harmonic	Root: _____	Quality: _____
The Supertonic Triad of g sharp minor harmonic	Root: _____	Quality: _____
The Subdominant Triad of G flat Major	Root: _____	Quality: _____
The Submediant Triad of F sharp Major	Root: _____	Quality: _____
The Tonic Triad of a sharp minor harmonic	Root: _____	Quality: _____

UltimateMusicTheory.com © Copyright 2013 Gloryland Publishing. All Rights Reserved.

ULTIMATE MUSIC THEORY
ADVANCED EXAM SET #1 - EXAM #4

10. Analyze the following musical excerpt by answering the questions below.

Minuet in G

Moderato

Ludwig van Beethoven
(1770 - 1827)

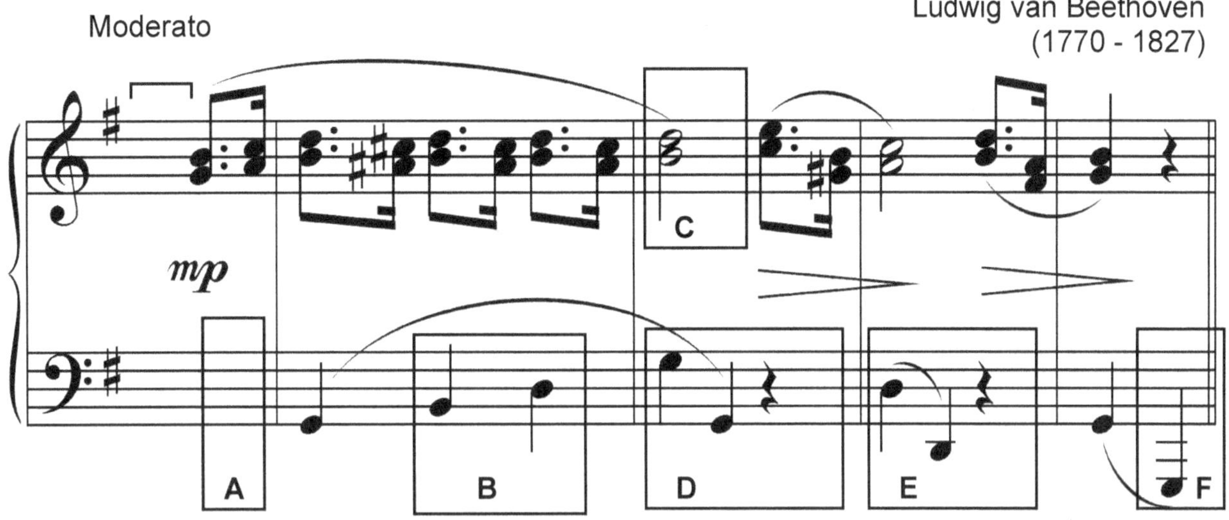

a) Name the Title of this excerpt. _____

b) Explain the tempo of this excerpt. _____

c) Name the Composer of this excerpt. _____

d) Name the year that the Composer was born in. _____

e) Add the Time Signature directly on the music.

f) Add the correct rest at the letter **A**.

g) Name the intervals at the letters: **B** _____ **C** _____

h) Name the relationship of the measures at **D** and **E**: _____

i) Identify the technical degree for the note at the letter **F**. _____

j) How many measures are in this excerpt? _____

 **Workbooks, Exams, Answers, Online Courses, App & More!**

A Proven Step-by-Step System to Learn Theory Faster - from Beginner to Advanced.

Innovative techniques designed to develop a complete understanding of music theory, to enhance sight reading, ear training, creativity, composition and musical expression.

All UMT Series have matching Answer Books!

The UMT Rudiments Series - Beginner A, Beginner B, Beginner C, Prep 1, Prep 2, Basic, Intermediate, Advanced & Complete (All-In-One)

- ♪ 12 Lessons, Review Tests, and a Final Exam to develop confidence
- ♪ Music Theory Guide & Chart for fast and easy reference of theory concepts
- ♪ 80 Flashcards for fun drills to dramatically increase retention & comprehension

Rudiments Exam Series - Preparatory, Basic, Intermediate & Advanced

- ♪ 8 Exams plus UMT Tips on How to Score 100% on Theory Exams

Each Rudiments Workbook correlates to a Supplemental Workbook.

The UMT Supplemental Series - Prep Level, Level 1, Level 2, Level 3, Level 4, Level 5, Level 6, Level 7, Level 8 & Complete (All-In-One) Level

- ♪ Form & Analysis and Music History - Composers, Eras & Musical Styles
- ♪ Melody Writing using ICE - Imagine, Compose & Explore
- ♪ 12 Lessons, Review Tests, Final Exam and 80 Flashcards for quick study

Supplemental Exam Series - Level 5, Level 6, Level 7 & Level 8

- ♪ 8 Exams to successfully prepare for nationally recognized Theory Exams

UMT Online Courses, Music Theory App & More

- ♪ UMT Certification Course, Teachers Membership & Elite Educator Program
- ♪ Ultimate Music Theory App correlates to the Rudiments Workbooks
- ♪ Free Resources - Teachers Guide, Music Theory Blogs, videos & downloads

Go To: **UltimateMusicTheory.com**

www.ingramcontent.com/pod-product-compliance
Lightning Source LLC
Chambersburg PA
CBHW081734100526
44591CB00016B/2618